The Collegeville Prayer of the Faithful Annual, 2008

Cycle A

Michael Kwatera, O.S.B.

LITURGICAL PRESS

Collegeville, Minnesota

www.litpress.org

*Dedicated to the sisters of Saint Benedict's Monastery,
Saint Joseph, Minnesota,
as they celebrate
a hundred and fifty years
of prayer and work*

Contents

Liturgical Year A

Contents

Introduction

When Pope Urban IV asked Thomas Aquinas to compose the Divine Office and Mass texts for the newly-established feast of Corpus Christi (1264), the Dominican friar and theologian professed his unworthiness for so sacred a task. But he completed it beautifully. I am no Thomas Aquinas, yet I, too, feel humbled in preparing this collection of intercessory prayers for the eucharistic liturgy. To place prayerful words on human lips and in human hearts is a most sacred work.

My *Preparing the General Intercessions* (Liturgical Press, 1996) is a practical, "how-to" book for composing the Prayer of the Faithful for the Eucharist. This present volume is a collection of *almost* "ready-to-pray" intercessions for the Sundays, solemnities, and some civil holidays of the Lectionary's Cycle A. I say "almost," because every liturgist and/or pastor will want to include particular persons and needs in the texts found here. Also, matters of immediate concern (for example, local tragedies and natural disasters) will need to be included in these rather general texts. Often the intentions can be made more "local" by changing the persons to be prayed for. To facilitate this, a disk containing Microsoft Word files of these texts according to calendar dates has been included at the back of this volume.

Preparing prayers for the Christian assembly to pray is a challenging but rewarding task. It took some courage for the Catholic Church to permit clergy and laypersons to prepare the Prayer of the Faithful for their congregations rather than legislating mandatory texts for use by the entire church. Thus, the *General Instruction of the Roman Missal* (2000) states:

> It is for the priest celebrant to direct this prayer from the chair. He himself begins it with a brief introduction by which he invites the faithful to pray, and likewise he concludes it with a prayer. The intentions announced should be sober, be composed freely but prudently, and be succinct, and they should express the prayer of the entire community (no. 71).

This statement gives generous freedom to those who prepare the Prayer of the Faithful but also requires careful discipline and theological accuracy in composing this prayer. I hope that such qualities are reflected in the prayer texts offered here.

Annie Dillard wrote about her Congregationalist pastor:

> Once, in the middle of the long pastoral prayer of intercession for the whole world—for the gift of wisdom to its leaders, for hope and mercy to the grieving and pained, succor to the oppressed, and God's grace to all—in the middle of this he stopped, and burst out, "Lord, we bring you these same petitions every week." After a shocked pause, he continued reading the prayer. Because of this, I like him very much.[1]

The church must pray for the same things every week, because the same human needs are old and new every Sunday in different persons. But these needs can be presented to God in fresh language shaped by the liturgical feasts, seasons, and the Sunday Scripture readings, as I have tried to do in this collection. Robert W. Hovda puts it very well: "The general intercessions are not there to impress the world with our knowledge of what is best for everybody. They are there to help worshipers rely more heavily on God's word and on God's Spirit than our own devices—or on the mass media."[2]

In preparing the intentions, I have searched the day's Scripture readings, and especially the responsorial psalm, for a word or phrase that leaps out from the text. Such a word or phrase has often been used in each of the intentions, repeated again and again as the series unfolds. This serves to link the Prayer of the Faithful to the prayer of the psalm. In this way, a pattern is developed that draws the worshipers into the intentions and provides a certain rhythmic, lyrical quality to them.

As an example of this method, let us turn to the intentions for the Seventeenth Sunday in Ordinary Time (Cycle A) included here:

---

[1] Annie Dillard, *Holy the Firm* (New York: Harper & Row, Publishers, 1977) 58–59.

[2] Robert W. Hovda, "Real and Worshipful Intercessions," Amen Corner, in *Worship* 60, no. 6 (November 1986) 533.

Minister: That the merciful love of God
will come to all who serve the church
and comfort them in difficulty,
let us pray to the Lord:

That the saving wisdom of God
will come to rulers of nations and
communities
and shape their thoughts and actions for
peace,
let us pray to the Lord:

That the tender compassion of God
will come to those oppressed by any need
and renew their hope in God's promises,
let us pray to the Lord:

That the abundant healing of God
will come to the sick
and raise them up to wholeness of mind and
body,
let us pray to the Lord:

That the infinite power of God
will come to us gathered here
and sustain us in the way of God's commands,
let us pray to the Lord:

That the eternal happiness of God
will come to those who have died,
especially _____ and _____,
and be their treasure for ever,
let us pray to the Lord:

These intentions follow the order given in the *General Instruction of the Roman Missal* (2000):

    a. For the needs of the Church;
    b. For public authorities and the salvation of the whole world;
    c. For those burdened by any kind of difficulty;
    d. For the local community (no. 70).

The pattern in these intentions is: That the *something* of God will come to *someone* and do *something* for them, let us pray to the Lord. Additions to this set of intercessions should follow this pattern for the sake of consistency. The pattern in each set of intentions should be easily discernible. This will be helpful as particular intentions are needed, for example, praying for first communicants and confirmation candidates, as well as for inviting the assembly to include their personal needs and intentions, if desired. Many of the sets of intentions in this book conclude with such an invitation. Presenting these additions in sense lines, as has been done in this book, will help lectors to proclaim these texts in the assembly.

Pope Benedict XVI has identified the intercessions as one of the liturgical "opportunities calling for the application of creativity."[3] Thus, the contribution of persons who have the gift of formulating intercessions should be encouraged. This task is properly the work of one gifted person for each occasion. "May he or she be a poet first," says Robert Hovda. "Any other qualifications are secondary."[4] Yes, a poet, because the Greek word "poet" means "creator." Preparing the Prayer of the Faithful is a craft in the service of the liturgy that requires divine assistance, human skill, and the fruitful creativity in which both work together.

Michael Kwatera, O.S.B.
June 24, 2007
Solemnity of the Birth of John the Baptist
in the sesquicentennial year of Saint John's Abbey

[3] Joseph Cardinal Ratzinger, "Structure of the Liturgical Celebration," in his *The Feast of Faith: Approaches to a Theology of the Liturgy*, trans. Graham Harrison (San Francisco: Ignatius Press, 1986) 68.
[4] Robert W. Hovda, "The Prayer of General Intercession," *Worship* 44, no. 8 (October 1970) 502.

FIRST SUNDAY OF ADVENT

Priest: As we begin the season of Advent,
we place our confidence in that glory begun
in us
by Christ's first coming,
and claim the hope for that perfection to be
accomplished in us
at his final coming.
May all people know Christ's many comings
in answer to these petitions.

Minister: That the leaders of the church will know
Christ's coming
as they promote unity among Christians,
let us pray to the Lord:

That the leaders of nations will know Christ's
coming
as they work to end oppression and violence,
let us pray to the Lord:

That the unemployed will know Christ's
coming
as they find opportunities for fruitful work,
let us pray to the Lord:

That the sick,
especially _____ and _____,
will know Christ's coming
as they receive the kindness of their sisters
and brothers,
let us pray to the Lord:

That we will know Christ's coming in one
        another
as we receive him in this Eucharist,
let us pray to the Lord:

That those who have died,
especially _____ and _____,
will know Christ's coming
as they celebrate life with him for ever,
let us pray to the Lord:

+

+

Priest: Lord God, your loving kindness enables us to
        find your Son
wherever he comes to us:
in his Word, in this meal, and in our brothers
        and sisters.
Let our prayers at this Eucharist
prepare us to welcome him at the end of time,
when he will be revealed as the Lord of glory,
for ever and ever. Amen.

IMMACULATE CONCEPTION

Priest: The sinless Virgin Mary is God's delight
from all eternity,
and the church's advocate in every age.
As we honor her immaculate conception,
let us join our prayers to hers.

Minister: With holy Mary, mother of Christians,
let us ask unity for the holy church of God
throughout the world.
For this, let us pray to the Lord:

With holy Mary, child of our father Abraham,
let us ask peace for all his descendants
in the Middle East.
For this, let us pray to the Lord:

With holy Mary, helper of the afflicted,
let us ask deliverance from pain and sorrow.
For this, let us pray to the Lord:

With holy Mary, bride of the Holy Spirit,
let us ask the Spirit's power in our lives
these Advent days.
For this, let us pray to the Lord:

With holy Mary, mother of the Son of God,
let us ask eternal life with him
for all who have died,
especially _____ and _____.
For this, let us pray to the Lord:

+

+

Priest: **God of endless ages,
your Holy Spirit prepared the Blessed Virgin
       Mary
to be a worthy dwelling for your Son.
Through her prayers, offered with ours,
grant what we need to live as her children
and bring us to the glory of your eternal home.
We ask this through Christ our Lord. Amen.**

SECOND SUNDAY OF ADVENT

Priest: The Lord Jesus is always near to us,
always coming into our hearts.
As we await the revelation of Christ's glory
at the end of the ages,
let us ask the Father to hear and answer the
     prayers we make
in the name of the beloved Son.

Minister: That the Lord will give wisdom
to those who shepherd and teach the church,
let us pray to the Lord:

That the Lord will give comfort
to those who live in the agony of warfare and
     violence,
let us pray to the Lord:

That the Lord will give healing
to those who are weakened by sickness,
especially _____ and _____,
let us pray to the Lord:

That the Lord will give perseverance
to those who are persecuted for their witness
     to the truth,
let us pray to the Lord:

That the Lord will give salvation
to those who have died,
especially _____ and _____,
let us pray to the Lord:

+

+

Priest: Lord God, ruler of all times and seasons,
we ask you to fill these days of waiting with
your saving love.
Help us grow in our love for you
and for each other,
and be at peace in your sight.
Bring us to glory with Jesus Christ,
who lives and reigns with you and the Holy
Spirit,
one God, for ever and ever. Amen.

December 12, 2007

OUR LADY OF GUADALUPE
(United States of America)

Priest: In our Lady of Guadalupe,
the desert of our human sorrow
blooms with God's abundant consolation.
As we honor her on this festival day,
let us pray for her children everywhere.

Minister: For the welfare of the holy churches of God
and the unity of humankind,
let us pray to the Lord:

For the well-being and prosperity
of all the peoples of the Americas,
let us pray to the Lord:

For the recovery of the sick,
especially _____ and _____,
and the liberation of the oppressed,
let us pray to the Lord:

For our deliverance from hostility
and protection from danger,
let us pray to the Lord:

For eternal life and everlasting joy
for those who have died,
especially _____ and _____,
let us pray to the Lord:

+

+

Priest: **Lord God,**
in the Son of the Blessed Virgin Mary
you have reconciled things earthly and
heavenly.
Through our prayers,
we commend ourselves, one another,
and our whole life to you,
and ask to stand with Mary in the light of
your glory,
for ever and ever. Amen.

December 16, 2007

THIRD SUNDAY OF ADVENT

Priest: My brothers and sisters,
let us rejoice heartily in the Lord Jesus Christ,
through whom the world was made in the
beginning
and through whom it will be renewed
at the end of time.
Filled with confidence in God's promised
salvation,
let us present these petitions
to the Giver of every blessing.

Minister: For Christian churches and communities,
that the Lord's glad tidings
will renew them in their words and deeds of
discipleship,
let us pray to the Lord:

For leaders of governments,
that the Lord's glad tidings
will guide them in the ways of justice and
peace,
let us pray to the Lord:

For the sick,
that the Lord's glad tidings
will heal them in mind and body,
let us pray to the Lord:

For babies about to be born,
that the Lord's glad tidings
will bring them to the fullness of their
        humanity,
let us pray to the Lord:

For this assembly of God's people,
that the Lord's glad tidings
will make us a source of spiritual joy for each
        other,
let us pray to the Lord:

For those who have died,
especially _____ and _____,
that the Lord's glad tidings
will be their everlasting joy,
let us pray to the Lord:

+

+

Priest: Lord God,
              you have promised to renew all creation:
              the world of nature and the world of the spirit.
              Answer our prayers for enduring joy and
                      gladness in Christ Jesus,
              for he is near us now,
              and will be with us in the world to come,
              for ever and ever. Amen.

FOURTH SUNDAY OF ADVENT

Priest: My sisters and brothers, with Mary and
            Joseph
            we know that all things are possible with God
            and so we confidently ask the Lord to hear our
            prayers.

Minister: That the servants of Jesus Christ
             will receive the Lord's blessing
             in living the Gospel,
             let us pray to the Lord:

             That local, state, and national officials
             will receive the Lord's blessing
             in doing justice for all in need,
             let us pray to the Lord:

             That pregnant women
             will receive the Lord's blessing
             in the birth of their children,
             let us pray to the Lord:

             That those facing decisions about their future
             will receive the Lord's blessing
             in seeking God's will,
             let us pray to the Lord:

             That we who prepare to celebrate Christmas
             will receive the Lord's blessing
             in serving others,
             let us pray to the Lord:

That those who have died,
especially _____ and _____,
will receive the Lord's blessing
in living with God for ever,
let us pray to the Lord:

+

+

Priest: God of Mary and Joseph, and our God,
we ask you to answer these prayers,
for we pray only that your will
be done in us and through us.
Let your blessing be powerfully present
in every word we speak and in every action
       we perform for your glory.
We ask this through Christ our Lord. Amen.

CHRISTMAS EVE

Priest: In deepest night, the light of God shines
        brightest
in our Savior, Christ the Lord.
Let us place our hope in him
as we pray in his name,
asking that God's salvation
will reach the ends of the earth.

Minister: That all members of the church
be renewed by the loving mercy of our God,
let us pray to the Lord:

That all who seek security or advantage
by means of violence
be converted to seeking the peace of our God,
let us pray to the Lord:

That unemployed, impoverished, and
        marginalized persons,
here in our midst and far away,
find deliverance in the justice of our God,
let us pray to the Lord:

That all who suffer from disease and injury,
especially _____ and _____,
know the healing love of our God,
let us pray to the Lord:

That all who worship here,
weighed down by the yoke of our sinfulness,
rejoice in the liberating power of our God,
let us pray to the Lord:

That those who have died,
especially _____ and _____,
live for ever in the radiant glory of our God,
let us pray to the Lord:

+

+

Priest: God of glory,
we know your zeal for our salvation
in the birth of our Savior, Jesus Christ.
Let the grace we find in him
become the answer to our prayers,
this day and every day,
both now and for ever. Amen.

CHRISTMAS DAY

Priest: This day our God came among us a tiny child
to show us the saving power of divine love.
Let us pray for the fullness of God's grace and
truth
in ourselves and in all people,
even to the ends of the earth.

Minister: That Jesus, Word of God made flesh,
be God's joy for all members of the church,
let us pray to the Lord:

That Jesus, desire of nations,
be God's peace among states and peoples,
let us pray to the Lord:

That Jesus, consolation of all hearts,
be God's healing and strength for those
in need,
let us pray to the Lord:

That Jesus, Savior of the world,
be God's light in our darkness,
let us pray to the Lord:

That Jesus, king of blessedness,
be God's everlasting happiness
for those who have died,
especially _____ and _____,
let us pray to the Lord:

+

+

Priest: **Lord God,
let your Son, born for us this day,
announce peace and good news to our world
in answer to these prayers.
Yours be the praise and the glory,
here on earth and in highest heaven,
both now and for ever. Amen.**

HOLY FAMILY OF JESUS, MARY, AND JOSEPH

Priest: As we seek to walk together in the Lord's
ways,
let us ask God's grace in all we say and do as
God's family.

Minister: That all who are God's chosen ones by
baptism
may be one in God's holy church,
let us pray to the Lord:

That all who fear the Lord,
of every nation and people,
may be one in their search for peace and
justice,
let us pray to the Lord:

That Christian families may be one
in every virtue and mutual forgiveness,
let us pray to the Lord:

That all who are separated or estranged
from their relatives during this holy season
may be one in God's love,
let us pray to the Lord:

That those who have died,
especially _____ and _____,
may for ever be one in God's new Jerusalem,
let us pray to the Lord:

+

+

Priest: **Almighty Father,**
you sent your Son among us
to bring us your joy and peace.
Through these prayers, increase that joy
    and peace
in every human heart,
and multiply your blessings among us
for our good and your glory,
both now and for ever. Amen.

MARY, MOTHER OF GOD

Priest: Through Jesus Christ, born of the Virgin
Mary,
let us welcome the year of our Lord
two thousand and eight
by turning to God in fervent prayer.

Minister: That those who serve the church
will know God's gracious love in their
ministry,
let us pray to the Lord:

That leaders of governments
and all peoples of the earth
will know God's peace and justice in their
communities,
let us pray to the Lord:

That those who face the future with anxiety
will know God's consolation in their fears,
let us pray to the Lord:

That we who are called to live as heirs of God
will know God's blessing in our lives,
let us pray to the Lord:

That those who have died,
especially _____ and _____,
will know God's salvation in their eternal
home,
let us pray to the Lord:

+

+

Priest: **Lord our God,**
by the help of Mary's prayers,
keep us faithful in your service
during this new year that you give us,
and let our words and actions
give glory to your name.
We ask this through Christ our Lord. Amen.

EPIPHANY OF THE LORD

Priest: **Let us bring our prayers to the God of glory,
who fulfills our hopes in the birth of the
beloved Son.**

Minister: **That the church will announce God's salvation
to the ends of the earth,
let us pray to the Lord:**

**That the citizens of all nations
will hallow God's name in peace,
let us pray to the Lord:**

**That immigrants and exiles will rejoice in
God's promise
of justice and consolation,
let us pray to the Lord:**

**That those weakened by sin and sickness
will find strength in God's healing,
let us pray to the Lord:**

**That we will show forth God's glory
by lives of holiness,
let us pray to the Lord:**

**That those who have died,
especially _____ and _____,
will know everlasting joy
in proclaiming God's praise,
let us pray to the Lord:**

+

+

Priest: Lord,
we join with every nation to adore you,
for like the Magi, we find our everlasting light
    in your Son
who dwells with us.
Let his glory fill the earth
as his presence fills our lives.
Answer our prayers for your saving help,
and sustain us in your justice.
We ask this through Christ our Lord. Amen.

BAPTISM OF THE LORD

Priest: Gathered as God's holy people,
let us offer prayer for all in need,
both in this community and throughout all
the world.

Minister: That the church, born of water and the Spirit,
may be filled with new power for good,
let us pray to the Lord:

That people of every nation
may be cleansed from hatred and violence,
let us pray to the Lord:

That those who suffer in body, mind, or spirit
may be freed from every evil,
let us pray to the Lord:

That we who form one people in Jesus Christ
may be made more perfectly like him,
let us pray to the Lord:

That those who have died
marked with the sign of faith,
especially _____ and _____,
may be reborn to eternal life,
let us pray to the Lord:

+

+

Priest: **Lord,
you empower those who have been baptized
to announce the good news of salvation
to people everywhere.
Hear and answer our prayers
to fulfill our baptismal mission,
so that all may live as your children,
brothers and sisters of Jesus Christ,
who is Lord for ever and ever. Amen.**

SECOND SUNDAY IN ORDINARY TIME

Priest: The love of God embraces all peoples;
God's kindness knows no limit.
Let us place our hope in God
as we offer these petitions.

Minister: For the shepherds and guardians of the
    church,
let us pray to the Lord:

For those who work for the unity of all
    Christians,
let us pray to the Lord:

For those who are considering an abortion,
let us pray to the Lord:

For those who defend the sanctity of human
    life,
let us pray to the Lord:

For all who are hungry, homeless, or exploited
    by the powerful of this world,
let us pray to the Lord:

For our relatives and friends who are ill,
let us pray to the Lord:

For those who are dying
with no one to comfort them,
let us pray to the Lord:

For those who have died in the peace of Christ,
especially _____ and _____,
let us pray to the Lord:

+

+

Priest: **God of our strength, hear our prayers.**
         May our oneness with you and each other
         be the living sign of your presence
         in our divided world.
         We ask this through Christ our Lord. Amen.

REV. DR. MARTIN LUTHER KING, JR.
(United States of America)

Priest: In Dr. Martin Luther King, Jr.,
the truth shines forth:
there is no greater love
than to give one's life for one's friends.
On this day of remembrance,
let us pray for the grace
to love God and neighbor as he did.

Minister: That Christians receive power
to suffer for the sake of conscience,
let us pray to the Lord:

That public officials receive courage
to oppose injustice and promote equality,
let us pray to the Lord:

That prophets in our midst receive strength
to glory in the cross of persecution,
let us pray to the Lord:

That we receive deliverance
from all sin and from fear of death,
let us pray to the Lord:

That those who have died,
especially _____ and _____,
receive everlasting life with Jesus Christ,
the faithful witness,
let us pray to the Lord:

+

+

Priest: **God of martyrs,
hear our prayers as we give thanks
for the ministry of Dr. Martin Luther King, Jr.,
so that his dream may give us hope
and transform our world for your glory,
both now and for ever. Amen.**

THIRD SUNDAY IN ORDINARY TIME

Priest: Let us turn to God in our need,
trusting in God's goodness and mercy.

Minister: For the leaders of the churches,
that they help all Christians to bear the fruit
    of the Spirit
in unity and love,
let us pray to the Lord:

For President Bush and Vice-President Cheney,
for members of the Cabinet and the Congress,
and for the justices of the Supreme Court,
that they protect the rights of all people,
let us pray to the Lord:

For expectant parents,
that they receive abundant strength and joy
in God's gift of life,
let us pray to the Lord:

For ourselves,
that we live in the light of the risen Christ
and accept his call to follow him,
let us pray to the Lord:

For those who have died,
especially _____ and _____,
that they celebrate everlasting life
with the Creator and Redeemer of all,
let us pray to the Lord:

✠

✠

Priest: God of the living,
            you have called us to walk the way of unity
                and peace.
            Confirm us in our hope that life is mightier
                than death,
            and, in answer to our prayers,
            let us know the great power for good
            that flows from your Son's resurrection.
            We ask this through Christ our Lord. Amen.

FOURTH SUNDAY IN ORDINARY TIME

Priest: **Let us humbly take refuge in the name of the Lord
as we offer our petitions.**

Minister: **That Jesus, the wisdom of God,
will enlighten the church for proclaiming the reign of God,
let us pray to the Lord:**

**That Jesus, the righteousness of God,
will guide world leaders into the ways of peace and justice,
let us pray to the Lord:**

**That Jesus, the consolation of God,
will raise up the needy by our care for them,
let us pray to the Lord:**

**That Jesus, the sanctification of God,
will make us holy and blessed in doing God's will,
let us pray to the Lord:**

**That Jesus, the salvation of God,
will welcome the dead into his kingdom,
especially _____ and _____,
let us pray to the Lord:**

+

+

Priest:　Ever-faithful God,
we seek you in the midst of this assembly
and in the heart of our world.
As we call upon your name in these prayers,
answer them for the sake of your beloved Son,
　Jesus Christ,
who is Lord for ever and ever. Amen.

ASH WEDNESDAY

Priest: With trust in God's merciful love and faithful
care,
let us present our needs in these prayers.

Minister: For the unity, peace, and welfare of the church
of God
on its way to holy Easter,
let us pray to the Lord:

For the perseverance of those soon to receive
the Easter sacraments,
let us pray to the Lord:

For the elimination of slavery, exploitation,
and conflict
in human hearts and in our world,
let us pray to the Lord:

For the spiritual gifts we need
to fulfill our mission as ambassadors for
Christ,
let us pray to the Lord:

For the grace to pray, fast, and serve the needy
as the Lord wills,
let us pray to the Lord:

For the happiness
of those called to share God's eternal day of
salvation,
especially _____ and _____,
let us pray to the Lord:

+

+

Priest: **Giver of forgiveness,
hear our prayers for your merciful love
as we enter this season of repentance.
Let our fasting from sin
become our feasting on your Easter glory
in Jesus Christ,
who is Lord for ever and ever. Amen.**

FIRST SUNDAY OF LENT
(World Marriage Day)

Priest: In the spirit of Jesus,
who offered fervent prayer to his Father in
     the desert,
let us call upon the God of mercy.

Minister: That hesitation and doubt in those chosen
     today
for Christian initiation at Easter,
especially _____ and _____,
be taken away by God's faithfulness,
let us pray to the Lord:

That lukewarmness in our discipleship
be overcome by God's Holy Spirit,
let us pray to the Lord:

That poverty and injustice in this land and
     every land
be ended by God's compassion in human
     hearts,
let us pray to the Lord:

That on this World Marriage Day,
the commitment of wives and husbands
be renewed by God's grace,
let us pray to the Lord:

That the death of our loved ones,
especially _____ and _____,
be turned into everlasting life by God's gift,
let us pray to the Lord:

+

+

Priest: **Lord God,**
you created Adam and Eve for your glory,
but they turned away from your love.
Now you have re-created us, their
    descendants,
through the obedience of your beloved Son.
In his name, we ask you to answer our
    prayers,
so that we may love you with all our hearts,
and do all that his Gospel requires of us.
Grant this through Christ our Lord. Amen.

SECOND SUNDAY OF LENT

Priest: Let us call upon the God of our ancestors,
              who is rich in compassion and love
              toward every generation.

Minister: That the Lord's mercy be upon the church
              and be its strength,
              let us pray to the Lord:

              That the Lord's mercy be upon
                  candidates for reception into full
                  communion of the Catholic Church
              especially _____ and _____,
              and be their promise of salvation,
              let us pray to the Lord:

              That the Lord's mercy be upon nations and
                  peoples,
              especially the children of Abraham,
              and be their source of justice and peace,
              let us pray to the Lord:

              That the Lord's mercy be upon all who are
                  alienated from God and others,
              and be their bond of love,
              let us pray to the Lord:

              That the Lord's mercy be upon us who are
                  saved by Jesus Christ,
              and be our hope in every difficulty,
              let us pray to the Lord:

That the Lord's mercy be upon those who
      have died,
especially _____ and _____,
and be their gift of immortality,
let us pray to the Lord:

+

+

Priest: **Father of glory,**
you sent your beloved Son, Jesus Christ,
to redeem us from sin and lead us to holiness.
Answer our prayers,
so that we may receive your mercy
and share it with others.
We ask this through the same Christ our Lord.
      Amen.

THIRD SUNDAY OF LENT

Priest: My sisters and brothers,
          we are gathered during this holy season of
               repentance
          to celebrate the mystery of our salvation in
               Jesus Christ.
          Let us ask our merciful God to open for all
               the world
          this fountain of life and blessing.

Minister: For all church leaders,
          that their work be blessed and made fruitful,
          let us pray to the Lord:

          For those who are preparing for Christian
               initiation at Easter,
          especially _____ and _____,
          that they look forward to this celebration with
               fervent joy,
          let us pray to the Lord:

          For the leaders of our country and of every
               nation,
          that they work together to meet the needs of
               the poor,
          let us pray to the Lord:

          For those who hunger and thirst for
               righteousness, justice, and peace,
          that they be satisfied,
          let us pray to the Lord:

For the ill, the aged, and the dying,
that their hope in God's merciful love
give them comfort and peace,
let us pray to the Lord:

For all of us who worship here,
that the love of God be abundantly poured
        into our hearts
so we may pour out that love to others,
let us pray to the Lord:

For those who have died,
especially _____ and _____,
that they rejoice for ever in the glory of God,
let us pray to the Lord:

+

+

Priest: Lord God, you are our Savior.
Let us draw water joyfully from the springs of
        your mercy
as did the woman of Samaria.
Grant us your saving help in answer to our
        prayers,
for we make them in the name of your Son,
Jesus Christ, who is Lord for ever and ever.
        Amen.

FOURTH SUNDAY OF LENT

Priest: Let us ask our God to illumine us and all
the world
with the light of Christ
in answer to these prayers.

Minister: That all the members of the church,
and those who are preparing to become
members at Easter,
especially _____ and _____,
will find renewed strength in God's mercy,
let us pray to the Lord:

That all people will find lasting peace in
God's will,
let us pray to the Lord:

That the blind and the ill, the infirm and the
dying,
will find abundant comfort in God's love,
let us pray to the Lord:

That all who worship here
will find welcome refreshment in God's
goodness,
let us pray to the Lord:

That those who have died,
especially _____ and _____,
will find everlasting happiness in God's
house,
let us pray to the Lord:

+

+

Priest: Lord God, unfailing light and Father of lights,
by the death and resurrection of Jesus Christ,
you have cast out the darkness of hatred and
    deceit,
and have poured out on the human family
the brightness of truth and love.
Answer the prayers we have made to you.
Help us to live as children of light,
this day and every day,
both now and for ever. Amen.

FIFTH SUNDAY OF LENT

Priest: Let us offer our fervent prayers to the
living God,
who makes us fully alive in Christ Jesus.

Minister: That the ministers of the church
will know the Spirit's power in their
self-sacrifice,
let us pray to the Lord:

That those who are preparing for baptism
[and for reception into the Catholic Church],
especially _____ and _____,
will know the Spirit's faithfulness
in their commitment to Christ,
let us pray to the Lord:

That the citizens of this and every land
will know the Spirit's peace
in their pursuit of justice,
let us pray to the Lord:

That we will know the Spirit's goodness
in our prayer, fasting, and works of charity,
let us pray to the Lord:

That those who have died,
especially _____ and _____,
will know the Spirit's joy in eternal life,
let us pray to the Lord:

+

+

Priest: God of the living,
your Son raised Lazarus from death
as a sign that he came to give us life in fullest
      measure.
By your Holy Spirit, fill us with life.
Renew our faith, hope, and love,
so that we may live with you always,
and come to share the glory of the
      resurrection.
We ask this through Christ our Lord. Amen.

ST. JOSEPH, HUSBAND OF THE BLESSED VIRGIN MARY
(transferred from March 19)

Priest: With faith in God's promises,
let us present our needs and petitions in
company with Saint Joseph.

Minister: That God's compassion will endure
as the heart of the church's ministry,
let us pray to the Lord:

That God's peace will endure
as the unity of nations and peoples,
let us pray to the Lord:

That God's salvation will endure
as healing for the sick and injured,
especially _____ and _____,
let us pray to the Lord:

That God's faithfulness will endure
as our hope in God's goodness,
let us pray to the Lord:

That God's kindness will endure
as eternal life for those who have died,
especially _____ and _____,
let us pray to the Lord:

+

+

Priest: **Blessed is Saint Joseph, O Lord,**
and all who dwell in your house.
Receive our prayers for the saving love
you have revealed in our Savior, Jesus
Christ,
who lives and reigns for ever and ever. Amen.

PALM SUNDAY OF THE LORD'S PASSION

Priest: Jesus Christ suffered for us and left us an
            example
            so that we could follow in his steps.
            Let us ask God to guide our saving passage
            through death to life
            in answer to these prayers.

Minister: For all who bear Christ's name,
            that they receive strength in the Lord
            who endured the cross,
            let us pray to the Lord:

            For the elect and candidates for full
            communion,
            especially _____ and _____,
            that they receive joy
            in knowing God's love and our love for them,
            let us pray to the Lord:

            For the people of this and every land,
            that they receive the blessings of justice and
            peace,
            let us pray to the Lord:

            For the sick, the elderly, and the dying,
            that they receive courage from the fidelity
            of God's Suffering Servant,
            let us pray to the Lord:

For us who enter upon this Holy Week,
that we receive salvation in confessing
that Jesus Christ is Lord,
let us pray to the Lord:

For those who have died,
especially _____ and _____,
that they receive everlasting glory
with their risen Savior,
let us pray to the Lord:

+

+

Priest: Lord God,
by the precious and life-giving Cross of your
  beloved Son,
answer our prayers for the salvation we find
  in him.
Let it be our strength in your service,
this Sunday and this Holy Week,
both now and for ever. Amen.

HOLY THURSDAY

Priest: Rejoicing in what we have received from the Lord—
a new and everlasting covenant in the Eucharist—
let us pray that this sacrifice of thanksgiving will bring God's life to all the world.

Minister: That the Eucharist, sacrament of our passover with Christ,
will nourish the church during these most holy days,
let us pray to the Lord:

That the Eucharist, fount of all graces,
will lead all peoples and nations
to know and love Christ the Lord,
let us pray to the Lord:

That the Eucharist, fruit of suffering and death,
will console all who suffer,
especially _____ and _____,
let us pray to the Lord:

That the Eucharist, bread of life and cup of salvation,
will be our memorial feast of joy,
let us pray to the Lord:

That the Eucharist, food of travelers from this
    world to the next,
will raise up to everlasting life
those who have died,
especially _____ and _____,
let us pray to the Lord:

+

+

Priest: Liberating God,
receive these prayers
as we proclaim the death of your Son, Jesus
    Christ.
Answer them for the sake of him
who loved his own in this world even to
    death,
and who loves us, his sisters and brothers,
both now and for ever. Amen.

HOLY SATURDAY: EASTER VIGIL

Priest: **Jesus Christ, risen from the dead,**
has made us alive for God, now and always.
In his most sacred name,
let us pray that his glorious triumph over sin
  and death
will be ours in answer to these prayers.

Minister: **That the holy and life-giving resurrection**
  of Jesus
will bring glorious joy to all believers,
especially those who have been initiated
and received into the church this night,
_____ and _____,
let us pray to the Lord:

That the holy and life-giving resurrection
  of Jesus
will bring lasting justice and peace to the
  world,
let us pray to the Lord:

That the holy and life-giving resurrection
  of Jesus
will bring abundant healing and strength to
  all in need,
especially _____ and _____,
let us pray to the Lord:

That the holy and life-giving resurrection
  of Jesus
will bring renewed hope to us who worship
  here,
let us pray to the Lord:

That the holy and life-giving resurrection
  of Jesus
will bring eternal happiness to those who
  have died,
especially _____ and _____,
let us pray to the Lord:

+

+

Priest: Wonderful in our eyes, O God,
is the resurrection of your beloved Son.
Answer our prayers for the sake of him
who underwent the torment of the cross
but now reigns as the King of glory,
for ever and ever. Amen.

EASTER SUNDAY:
THE RESURRECTION OF THE LORD

Priest: Christ Jesus, the source of our hope,
has been raised from the dead.
With thankful praise, let us offer these
    petitions.

Minister: For all who have been raised up with Christ
    in baptism,
especially _____ and _____,
that they rejoice in God's merciful love,
let us pray to the Lord:

For all who serve in public office,
that they rejoice in God's call for justice and
    peace,
let us pray to the Lord:

For those who suffer in body, mind, or spirit,
that they rejoice in God's deliverance,
let us pray to the Lord:

For this assembly ,
that we rejoice in God's triumph over sin and
    death,
let us pray to the Lord:

For those who have died,
especially _____ and _____,
that they rejoice in God's gift of eternal life,
let us pray to the Lord:

+

+

Priest: **Most merciful God,**
your loving plan of salvation finds its glorious
     fulfillment
in the resurrection of your Son, Jesus Christ.
Extend that saving power
throughout our lives and our world,
this Easter day and every day,
both now and for ever. Amen.

SECOND SUNDAY OF EASTER
(Divine Mercy Sunday)

Priest: Wonderful in our eyes is the resurrection of
    Jesus,
the Son of God and minister of divine mercy.
Let us pray to share even now
in the eternal inheritance we have in him.

Minister: That those who preach the risen Christ in
    word and deed
receive strength in Jesus Christ,
let us pray to the Lord:

That those reborn at Easter,
especially _____ and _____,
receive joy in Jesus Christ,
let us pray to the Lord:

That all nations receive salvation in Jesus
    Christ,
let us pray to the Lord:

That all who are hard-pressed by sickness
    and injury,
by famine and warfare,
receive deliverance in Jesus Christ,
let us pray to the Lord:

That we who praise God this day
receive hope in Jesus Christ,
let us pray to the Lord:

That those who have died,
especially _____ and _____,
receive everlasting life in Jesus Christ,
let us pray to the Lord:

+

+

Priest: **Lord,**
we ask you to increase our faith in your risen
   Son,
so that we will welcome your salvation
in answer to these prayers.
Praise, glory, and honor be yours,
now and at the revelation of Jesus Christ,
who is Lord for ever and ever. Amen.

March 31, 2008

ANNUNCIATION OF THE LORD
(transferred from March 25)

Priest: Coming among us to do God's will,
Jesus Christ destroyed our death
and made us alive for God.
With Easter joy,
let us offer our petitions to the God who
saves.

Minister: That God will be with the members of the
church
in their words and deeds,
let us pray to the Lord:

That God will be with government officials
in their planning and decisions,
let us pray to the Lord:

That God will be with those who suffer
in their deliverance from poverty, illness, and
prejudice,
let us pray to the Lord:

That God will be with us
in the Word made flesh for our salvation,
let us pray to the Lord:

That God will be with those who have died,
especially _____ and _____,
in the assembly of God's holy ones,
let us pray to the Lord:

+

+

Priest: **Lord God,**
your Son, Jesus Christ, was born of the Virgin
    Mary
to consecrate us in your truth.
Unite our prayers to hers,
and make us, like her,
hearers of your Word and doers of your will.
We ask this through the same Christ our Lord.
    Amen.

THIRD SUNDAY OF EASTER

Priest: When we are discouraged, God consoles us.
When we are troubled, God is with us to help us.
In grateful confidence, let us ask God to hear our petitions.

Minister: That the church will powerfully proclaim to all people
the hope which the risen Christ gives them,
let us pray to the Lord:

That Christ's message of peace
will remove the pain of war and violence from human hearts,
let us pray to the Lord:

That we will use the fruits of the earth
according to God's plan,
and thus help to restore all things in Christ,
let us pray to the Lord:

That we will recognize and give thanks to the risen Lord
in the breaking of the bread
and wherever he reveals himself,
let us pray to the Lord:

That those who have died,
especially _____ and _____,
will rejoice for ever in the glory of the risen Christ,
let us pray to the Lord:

+

+

Priest: **Father,
truly your voice speaks of peace:
peace for us, your people,
and for all who turn to you in their hearts.
May our prayers at this Eucharist strengthen us
to be more worthy and grateful bearers of
    your peace to others.
We ask this in the name of Jesus the Lord.
    Amen.**

April 13, 2008

FOURTH SUNDAY OF EASTER

Priest: With hearts filled with Easter joy,
let us bring our prayers to the God
who raised Jesus from the dead.

Minister: That those who shepherd the holy church
of God
will find courage in the name of Jesus Christ,
let us pray to the Lord:

That those baptized at Easter,
especially our fellow parishioners,
_____ and _____,
will find lasting peace in the name of Jesus
Christ,
let us pray to the Lord:

That those who are crushed by sadness, pain,
and disappointment
will find joy in the name of Jesus Christ,
let us pray to the Lord:

That those who suffer from disability or
injury
will find strength in the name of Jesus Christ,
let us pray to the Lord:

That those who lack sufficient food or
adequate housing
will find bountiful help in the name of Jesus
Christ,
let us pray to the Lord:

That those who have died,
especially _____ and _____,
will find eternal life in the name of Jesus
    Christ,
let us pray to the Lord:

+

+

Priest: Lord God,
in the power of Jesus' name
we stand before you in fervent prayer.
Grant us and all your children
the salvation Christ won for us by his death
    and resurrection.
Keep us safe in his love,
and help us follow him to glory.
Let us dwell in your house,
at home with you, for ever and ever. Amen.

FIFTH SUNDAY OF EASTER

Priest: In Christ Jesus, dead and risen,
we recognize the saving plan of God
and come to believe in the power of God's
   redeeming love.
With Easter faith,
let us present our prayers to the God of mercy.

Minister: That the Christian churches may persevere in
   faith
and bear witness to the unifying power of the
   Holy Spirit,
let us pray to the Lord:

That nations and peoples
may rejoice in the blessings of peace and
   justice,
let us pray to the Lord:

That our suffering sisters and brothers,
especially the sick of our parish,
may have their sorrow turned into lasting joy,
let us pray to the Lord:

That our parish community
may build up the spiritual temple of God in
   our midst,
let us pray to the Lord:

That all who have died,
especially _____ and _____,
may enjoy fullness of life with the risen
   Christ,
let us pray to the Lord:

+

+

Priest: **Almighty God,**
we thank you for calling us to be a holy
   people
in Jesus Christ, our way, our truth, and our life.
Hear the prayers we offer,
so that we may speak his words and do his
   works
for the salvation of all.
We ask this through the same Christ our Lord.
   Amen.

SIXTH SUNDAY OF EASTER

Priest: Jesus has not left us orphans,
for he has sent the Holy Spirit to be with us
    always.
Through the power of the Spirit,
let us give voice to the needs of people
    everywhere
in these petitions.

Minister: That the church may persevere in works of
        justice and peace,
let us pray to the Lord:

That those who govern and exercise authority
may bring hope to the nations of the world,
let us pray to the Lord:

That the hungry and the homeless
may know the presence of Jesus Christ,
let us pray to the Lord:

That all parents, especially single parents,
may receive the strength and power of the
    Spirit
as they care for their children,
let us pray to the Lord:

That those who have gone before us in death,
especially _____ and _____,
may enter the place Christ has prepared for
    them,
let us pray to the Lord:

+

+

Priest: **We praise you, God of our joy, for your strong
bond of love
which unites us to your risen Son.
Give us your Spirit to help us in all our needs,
so that we may love in deed and in truth.
We ask this through Christ our Lord. Amen.**

ASCENSION OF THE LORD

(celebrated in some places on Sunday, May 4)

Priest: **Our Lord Jesus Christ,**
who took his seat at God's right hand,
remains with us and always works for our
good.
In his name, let us pray for our needs
and the needs of all people.

Minister: **That the victory of Jesus Christ over evil**
will fill the church with his saving power,
let us pray to the Lord:

That the compassion of Jesus Christ
will fill the leaders of governments with his
concern for others,
let us pray to the Lord:

That the presence of Jesus Christ
will fill the suffering with his consolation and
strength,
let us pray to the Lord:

That the Gospel of Jesus Christ
will fill this assembly with his zeal for service,
let us pray to the Lord:

That the mercy of Jesus Christ will fill those
who have died,
especially _____ and _____,
with his eternal glory,
let us pray to the Lord:

Let us remember our particular needs.

[pause for silent prayer]

**That the grace of Jesus Christ
will fill our lives with his abundant gifts,
let us pray to the Lord:**

+

+

Priest: **Father most holy,
we ask you to hear our prayers,
so that in the time between Jesus' ascension
and his return in majesty,
we may bear witness to your everlasting love
     for us.
We ask this in the name of him
who has ascended to your right hand,
there to celebrate life with you and the Holy
     Spirit,
for ever and ever. Amen.**

SEVENTH SUNDAY OF EASTER

(where the Ascension is celebrated on Thursday, May 1)

Priest: United in prayer with the Blessed Virgin Mary
and the apostles chosen by the Lord,
let us ask God for what we need this day.

Minister: For deeper faith in all the members of the
church,
and for the support of those baptized at Easter,
especially _____ and _____,
let us pray to the Lord:

For the well-being of this nation and its
government,
and for the safety of all who serve and protect
us,
let us pray to the Lord:

For the comforting of those who suffer in
body, mind, and spirit,
and for peace for the dying,
let us pray to the Lord:

For the continuing work of creation,
and for the building of a more humane world,
let us pray to the Lord:

For the ministry of God's care and healing to
others at our hands,
and for abundant life in the reign of God,
let us pray to the Lord:

For eternal joy for the faithful departed,
especially _____ and _____,
and for consolation for all who mourn them,
let us pray to the Lord:

+

+

Priest: Lord,
            we ask to see your goodness in answer to
                these prayers.
            Bring us to glory with Jesus Christ
            in the land where all are alive for you,
            for ever and ever. Amen.

PENTECOST SUNDAY
(Mother's Day)

Priest: United in the Spirit who helps us to pray
    rightly,
let us ask God to renew us and the face of
    the earth
in answer to these prayers.

Minister: May the glory of the Lord
be seen in the mutual service of God's people.
For this, let us pray to the Lord:

May the glory of the Lord
be seen in justice and peace among all
    nations.
For this, let us pray to the Lord:

May the glory of the Lord
be seen in the dedication and care of mothers.
For this, let us pray to the Lord:

May the glory of the Lord
be seen in healing for the sick,
especially _____ and _____,
and in recovery for the injured,
especially _____ and _____.
For this, let us pray to the Lord:

May the glory of the Lord
be seen in our faith, hope, and love.
For this, let us pray to the Lord:

May the glory of the Lord
be seen in everlasting happiness
for those who have died,
especially _____ and _____.
For this, let us pray to the Lord:

+

+

Priest: God of glory, giver of all good gifts,
mercifully answer our prayers.
Grant that we may welcome your Holy Spirit,
and rejoice to proclaim, "Jesus is Lord,"
both now and for ever. Amen.

THE MOST HOLY TRINITY

Priest: Having heard the Word of God,
let us now call upon our Father, who made us,
the Son, who redeemed us,
and the Holy Spirit, who renews us,
as we present these petitions.

Minister: That God will guide the Christian churches
in their search for unity,
so that their oneness will show forth
the unity of Father, Son, and Holy Spirit,
let us pray to the Lord:

That God will strengthen civil authorities
in their efforts to establish justice and peace,
let us pray to the Lord:

That God will remove every fear from human
hearts
and fill them with that perfect love
which comes from God alone,
let us pray to the Lord:

That God will build up this community for
service,
let us pray to the Lord:

That God will help us who have gathered here
to grow in the life of the Holy Trinity
by our celebration of this Eucharist,
let us pray to the Lord:

That God will bring those who have died,
especially _____ and _____,
to share an eternal communion of love,
let us pray to the Lord:

+

+

Priest: Lord God,
have mercy on us and hear our prayers.
Let the love which unites the Persons of the
        Trinity
shape our lives and the lives of all people.
We ask this in the name of Jesus, your Son,
who celebrates life with you and the Holy
        Spirit,
one God, for ever and ever. Amen.

THE MOST HOLY BODY AND BLOOD OF CHRIST

Priest: Let us ask God, our guide and protector,
to be mindful of us in our need.

Minister: That those who lead the churches
will help us live as the one Body of Christ,
let us pray to the Lord:

That national and local government officials
will satisfy the human hunger for peace and
    justice,
let us pray to the Lord:

That those who suffer in body and spirit
will be gladdened by many signs of divine
    and human love for them,
let us pray to the Lord:

That this assembly will delight in Christ's gift
    of himself in the Eucharist,
let us pray to the Lord:

That the dead,
especially _____ and _____,
will be raised up to sing God's praise in
    heaven,
let us pray to the Lord:

+

+

Priest: **God our Father,**
nothing is lacking to those who love you.
As you fed your people with manna on their
  desert journey,
nourish us on our pilgrim way
with the living Word and the living bread, our
  Lord Jesus Christ.
Hear our prayers for new life in him,
this day and every day,
both now and for ever. Amen.

May 26, 2008

MEMORIAL DAY
(United States of America)

Priest: **Let us confidently pray to the God of mercy,
who raised the beloved Son from death
as the firstfruits of eternal life.**

Minister: **For the salvation of all who follow the Gospel
of Christ,
let us pray to the Lord:**

**For the reign of God in this world,
let us pray to the Lord:**

**For the safety of travelers this holiday
weekend,
let us pray to the Lord:**

**For a place of refreshment, light, and peace
for all who have died,
especially defenders of our country,
let us pray to the Lord:**

**For the final destruction of sin and the grave
by the power of the risen Christ,
let us pray to the Lord:**

+

+

Priest: God of the dead and the living,
in your kindness grant what we have asked
    of you,
for we commend ourselves, one another,
and all the faithful departed to your Son,
    Jesus Christ,
who is Lord for ever and ever. Amen.

SACRED HEART

Priest: The saving plan of God took flesh in Jesus
            Christ.
            In his most sacred name, let us offer our
            petitions.

Minister: That God's kindness in the heart of Jesus
             will be seen and heard in the mission of the
             church,
             let us pray to the Lord:

             That God's peace in the heart of Jesus
             will deliver the world from warfare and
             violence,
             let us pray to the Lord:

             That God's forgiveness in the heart of Jesus
             will bring enemies to forgive each other,
             let us pray to the Lord:

             That God's compassion in the heart of Jesus
             will heal the ills of all who suffer,
             let us pray to the Lord:

             That God's goodness in the heart of Jesus
             will refresh the lives of those who worship
             here,
             let us pray to the Lord:

             That God's mercy in the heart of Jesus
             will raise up all who have died,
             especially _____ and _____,
             let us pray to the Lord:

+

+

Priest: God of the covenant,
your faithfulness saves us from every danger.
We ask you to answer these prayers
for the sake of your only Son, Jesus Christ,
in whom we find all the treasures of your love,
for ever and ever. Amen.

NINTH SUNDAY IN ORDINARY TIME

Priest: Let us bring our prayers to the Lord,
who leads us and guides us on the way of
  salvation.

Minister: That all who are justified by faith in Christ
will receive God's blessing in renewed hope,
let us pray to the Lord:

That all nations and communities
will receive God's blessing in lasting peace,
let us pray to the Lord:

That all who face difficult situations
will receive God's blessing in speedy
  deliverance,
let us pray to the Lord:

That we who celebrate the Eucharist here
will receive God's blessing in faithful love,
let us pray to the Lord:

That those who have died,
especially _____ and _____,
will receive God's blessing in everlasting joy,
let us pray to the Lord:

+

+

Priest: **Lord, we call upon you,
our rock of safety in every age.
Answer our prayers for your abundant
blessings in Christ Jesus,
both now and for ever. Amen.**

TENTH SUNDAY IN ORDINARY TIME

Priest: Let us pray for our needs
and the needs of people everywhere.

Minister: That the saving power of God
will strengthen the church for words and
deeds of reconciliation,
let us pray to the Lord:

That the saving power of God
will draw nations and peoples to works of
justice and peace,
let us pray to the Lord:

That the saving power of God
will rescue the sick and the poor from their
distress,
let us pray to the Lord:

That the saving power of God
will remove from our lives whatever is
harmful
and give us whatever is helpful,
let us pray to the Lord:

That the saving power of God
will bring those who have died,
especially _____ and _____,
to the glory of the resurrection,
let us pray to the Lord:

+

+

Priest: Lord, like the apostle Matthew,
we find a welcome place at this table
with your Son, Jesus Christ.
In his most sacred name, we ask your
    promised help
in answer to these prayers,
so that your saving power may be ours,
both now and for ever. Amen.

ELEVENTH SUNDAY IN ORDINARY TIME
(Father's Day)

Priest: **Jesus Christ loved us and gave himself up
for us,
so that we might be put right with God.
Let us pray for ourselves and for all people.**

Minister: **That the leaders of the church will live
for God
by seeking the unity of all Christians,
let us pray to the Lord:**

**That the nations and peoples of the earth will
live for God
by embracing justice and peace,
let us pray to the Lord:**

**That fathers will live for God
by generously serving their families in love,
let us pray to the Lord:**

**That those oppressed by any need will live
for God
by believing firmly in Jesus Christ,
let us pray to the Lord:**

**That we who worship here will live for God
by forgiving each other from our hearts,
let us pray to the Lord:**

That all who have died,
especially _____ and _____,
will live for God
by sharing in Christ's resurrection,
let us pray to the Lord:

+

+

Priest: Lord, though we are sinners,
you have taken away our guilt.
Shelter us and all people in answer to our
      prayers,
so that we may rejoice in you,
both now and for ever. Amen.

June 22, 2008

TWELFTH SUNDAY IN ORDINARY TIME

Priest: Let us ask God for what we need this day and
              this week
              as we present these petitions.

Minister: For all who believe in Christ,
              that God's loving favor will be theirs,
              let us pray to the Lord:

              For people of all nations,
              that God's infinite mercy will be theirs,
              let us pray to the Lord:

              For the poor,
              that God's bountiful help will be theirs at
                  our hands,
              let us pray to the Lord:

              For all who suffer,
              that God's abundant kindness will be theirs,
              let us pray to the Lord:

              For travelers and vacationers,
              that God's constant protection will be theirs,
              let us pray to the Lord:

              For ourselves,
              that God's enduring strength will be ours,
              let us pray to the Lord:

              For those who have died,
              especially _____ and _____,
              that God's everlasting love will be theirs,
              let us pray to the Lord:

+

+

Priest: **Lord,**
with the prophet Jeremiah
we entrust our lives into your hands.
With Jesus your Son,
we place our trust in your care for us.
Let your grace overflow for us and for all
people
in answer to these prayers,
for we offer them in the name of Jesus Christ,
who is Lord for ever and ever. Amen.

NATIVITY OF ST. JOHN THE BAPTIST

Priest: Let us pray to our God,
asking that the example of John the Baptist
    may shape our lives.

Minister: That like John the Baptist,
we may know how to advance Christ's work
    in the world,
let us pray to the Lord:

That like John,
we may direct all our actions to the service of
    Christ,
let us pray to the Lord:

That like John,
we may bear with courage
every suffering that witness to Christ brings us,
let us pray to the Lord:

That like John,
we may rejoice in the reign of God
made incarnate in Jesus Christ,
let us pray to the Lord:

That like John,
those who have died,
especially _____ and _____,
may enjoy the peace promised to those
who seek Christ in all things,
let us pray to the Lord:

+

+

Priest: **Lord God, in the fullness of time**
you revealed yourself to John the Baptist
in the coming of your Son.
Through these prayers,
help us to be always ready
to welcome Jesus Christ here in our midst
and in our sisters and brothers.
We ask this through the same Christ our Lord.
Amen.

SAINTS PETER AND PAUL, APOSTLES

Priest: **With the holy apostles Peter and Paul,
let us bring our needs and the needs of all
    people to the Lord.**

Minister: **For the strength of the Catholic faith
that comes to us from the apostles,
let us pray to the Lord:**

**For God's blessing on people, parishes, and
    communities
that bear the name of Saints Peter and Paul,
let us pray to the Lord:**

**For the safety and success
of the missionary apostolate of the church,
even to the ends of the earth,
let us pray to the Lord:**

**For the preaching of the Gospel by word and
    deed,
let us pray to the Lord:**

**For the everlasting joy of those who have
    died,
especially _____ and _____,
let us pray to the Lord:**

**Let us ask the Lord to help, save, and defend us
as we remember our needs.**

[pause for silent prayer]

For the needs we hold in our hearts,
let us pray to the Lord:

+

+

Priest: Heavenly Father,
your risen Son commissioned his chosen
apostles
to preach the good news to all creation.
By the prayers of Saints Peter and Paul,
strengthen us with apostolic teaching
and empower us to be your faithful witnesses
in the world.
We ask this through Christ our Lord. Amen.

INDEPENDENCE DAY
(United States of America)

Priest: From God alone comes our salvation.
On this Independence Day,
let us pour out our hearts before the Lord in
 fervent prayer.

Minister: For the unity of the church in the United
 States,
and for a life-giving share in the gifts of God,
let us pray to the Lord:

For peace throughout the whole world,
and for the prosperity of the human family,
let us pray to the Lord:

For the safety of those who serve in the armed
 forces,
and the well-being of their families,
let us pray to the Lord:

For an end to every threat to human life,
and for the elimination of hunger and disease,
let us pray to the Lord:

For the recovery of the sick and the relief of
 the poor,
let us pray to the Lord:

For the blessings of good weather throughout
 these summer days,
and for bountiful crops,
let us pray to the Lord:

For the consolation of the dying,
and eternal life for those who have died,
especially _____ and _____,
let us pray to the Lord:

+

+

Priest: Rock of our strength,
you never forsake your people,
but remember them in your great love.
We place our trust in you,
and ask your generous blessings in Christ
      Jesus,
both now and for ever. Amen.

FOURTEENTH SUNDAY IN ORDINARY TIME

Priest: Let us humbly ask our Father, Lord of heaven
and earth,
to receive our prayers.

Minister: That the leaders of the church
will accept the yoke of Christ
through lives of gentle and humble service,
let us pray to the Lord:

That the leaders of this and every country
will banish war and promote peace
throughout the world,
let us pray to the Lord:

That all who are overworked and bear heavy
responsibilities
may find rest and refreshment,
let us pray to the Lord:

That all who worship here
may trust in Christ and learn discipleship
through his teaching,
let us pray to the Lord:

That those who have died,
especially _____ and _____,
will celebrate everlasting life in the reign
of God,
let us pray to the Lord:

+

+

Priest: **Most merciful Father,**
we ask you to hear the prayers of your church.
Comfort us with your peace,
bless us with your Spirit,
so that our faith and confidence in your Son
may endure all hardships.
We make this prayer through Jesus Christ,
who has revealed you to us.
A just Savior is he, for ever and ever. Amen.

July 13, 2008

FIFTEENTH SUNDAY IN ORDINARY TIME

Priest: Let us present our petitions to the Lord,
remembering our needs and the needs of
people everywhere.

Minister: For all believers,
that the Word of God give them courage to
correct injustice
and heal the wounds of hate,
let us pray to the Lord:

For young Christians,
especially those gathering
for World Youth Day this week,
that God's Holy Spirit be their
power for witness,
let us pray to the Lord:

For all farmers,
that good weather bring their crops to
maturity
and crown the year with God's bounty,
let us pray to the Lord:

For all who suffer in body, mind, or spirit,
that the sufferings of the present
lead them to the glory promised to us,
let us pray to the Lord:

For those who have died,
especially _____ and _____,
that they rejoice for ever at the heavenly
banquet,
let us pray to the Lord:

For our particular intentions, which we now remember.

[pause for silent prayer]

For all our needs, let us pray to the Lord:

+

+

Priest: Lord God, we ask you to receive our prayers
and answer them according to your great
mercy.
Grant that whatever our labors for your
kingdom will sow
may produce an abundant harvest for eternity.
We make this prayer through Christ our Lord.
Amen.

July 20, 2008

SIXTEENTH SUNDAY IN ORDINARY TIME

Priest: **In the power of the Spirit who helps us to
pray rightly,
let us call on our God who cares for us.**

Minister: **That believers in Jesus Christ will know the
Lord's kindness
in living the Gospel,
let us pray to the Lord:**

**That the human family will know the Lord's
kindness
in all that leads to peace and justice,
let us pray to the Lord:**

**That the poor, the sick, and the persecuted
will know the Lord's kindness
in their deliverance from suffering,
let us pray to the Lord:**

**That we who worship here will know the
Lord's kindness in this Eucharist,
let us pray to the Lord:**

**That those who have died,
especially _____ and _____,
will know the Lord's kindness in everlasting
life,
let us pray to the Lord:**

+

+

Priest: **Wondrous are your deeds, O God, in every
time and place.
May your will be done in answer to our
prayers,
so that we may receive your kindness
in what we need this day.
We ask this through Christ our Lord. Amen.**

SEVENTEENTH SUNDAY IN ORDINARY TIME

Priest: My sisters and brothers,
let us ask that we will find all things working
   for our good
in answer to these prayers.

Minister: That the merciful love of God
will come to all who serve the church
and comfort them in difficulty,
let us pray to the Lord:

That the saving wisdom of God
will come to rulers of nations and
   communities
and shape their thoughts and actions for
   peace,
let us pray to the Lord:

That the tender compassion of God
will come to those oppressed by any need
and renew their hope in God's promises,
let us pray to the Lord:

That the abundant healing of God
will come to the sick
and raise them up to wholeness of mind and
   body,
let us pray to the Lord:

That the infinite power of God
will come to us gathered here
and sustain us in the way of God's commands,
let us pray to the Lord:

That the eternal happiness of God
will come to those who have died,
especially _____ and _____,
and be their treasure for ever,
let us pray to the Lord:

+

+

Priest: Gracious God,
as we walk in the light of your face,
increase in us your many gifts for our
  well-being.
Let them become our way to eternal life
with your risen Son, Jesus Christ,
who is Lord for ever and ever. Amen.

EIGHTEENTH SUNDAY IN ORDINARY TIME

Priest: **Let us call on the Lord,**
who is near to us in every need.

Minister: **For those who serve the church,**
let us pray to the Lord:

For those who lead nations and communities,
let us pray to the Lord:

For those who suffer from hunger, illness,
      and injustice,
let us pray to the Lord:

For those who desire healing of body, mind,
      or spirit,
let us pray to the Lord:

For those who are traveling these summer
      days,
let us pray to the Lord:

For those who have died in Christ,
especially _____ and _____,
let us pray to the Lord:

+

+

Priest: **Lord God,**
multiply your blessings among us
as your Son multiplied the loaves and fishes.
Praise and thanksgiving be yours, now and
      always,
through Jesus Christ, our Lord. Amen.

August 10, 2008

NINETEENTH SUNDAY IN ORDINARY TIME

Priest: Placing our confidence in God's love,
let us ask for the blessings
that God promises us in the beloved Son.

Minister: That the ministers of the church will reflect
the Lord's kindness
in their service to God's people,
let us pray to the Lord:

That the leaders of nations will find the Lord's
salvation
in their efforts for the good of all,
let us pray to the Lord:

That the poor will know the Lord's justice
in our generous works of charity,
let us pray to the Lord:

That we who assemble here
will recognize the Lord's presence in our
worship,
let us pray to the Lord:

That those who have died,
especially _____ and _____,
will receive the Lord's embrace in everlasting
life,
let us pray to the Lord:

+

+

Priest: **Lord God, your Son leads us on the way of
peace.
Draw us to him in this Eucharist,
so that we may rejoice in him now,
and live with him in your presence,
for ever and ever. Amen.**

ASSUMPTION OF MARY

Priest: **Let us ask God to receive our petitions
in the throne room of heaven,
where the glorious Virgin Mary powerfully
        prays for us.**

Minister: **For servants of the church,
called to minister God's salvation,
let us pray to the Lord:**

**For public officials,
called to promote God's justice and peace,
let us pray to the Lord:**

**For the lowly of the earth,
called to share a place of honor with Jesus
        Christ,
let us pray to the Lord:**

**For us gathered here,
called to welcome Christ the Lord in this
        Eucharist,
let us pray to the Lord:**

**For those who have died,
called to receive the mercy of God,
especially _____ and _____,
let us pray to the Lord:**

+

+

Priest: God of Elizabeth and Mary,
great were your saving deeds in their lives;
great is your merciful care in ours.
Come to our help in answer to these prayers,
for we offer them in the name of Jesus Christ,
your Anointed One,
who is Lord for ever and ever. Amen.

TWENTIETH SUNDAY IN ORDINARY TIME

Priest: Gathered in this house of prayer,
let us call upon our God.

Minister: That Jews, Christians, and Muslims, and all
people of faith
may find renewed strength in God's mercy,
let us pray to the Lord:

That all nations and peoples may find lasting
peace
in God's guidance,
let us pray to the Lord:

That the ill, the infirm, and the dying
may find abundant comfort in God's
deliverance,
let us pray to the Lord:

That all who worship here
may find welcome joy in God's gifts,
let us pray to the Lord:

That those who have died,
especially _____ and _____,
may find everlasting glory in God's salvation,
let us pray to the Lord:

+

+

Priest: **Lord,
with the persistence of the Canaanite woman
we boldly call out our needs,
for you always listen to the prayers of your
 people.
Grant us your generous blessings in Christ
 Jesus,
both now and for ever. Amen.**

TWENTY-FIRST SUNDAY IN ORDINARY TIME

Priest: **The love of the Lord is eternal.**
Let us ask the Lord to give us and all people
whatever is for our good.

Minister: **That the Lord will show great kindness**
to the leaders of the church,
and sustain them in their call to service,
let us pray to the Lord:

That the Lord will show great kindness
to the rulers of nations,
and strengthen them in their commitment
to justice,
let us pray to the Lord:

That the Lord will show great kindness
to the victims of poverty and prejudice,
and answer their cries for help,
let us pray to the Lord:

That the Lord will show great kindness
to those who have died,
especially _____ and _____,
and raise them up to everlasting life,
let us pray to the Lord:

That the Lord will show great kindness to us
as we remember our needs.

[pause for silent prayer]

That the Lord will grant us whatever is
     helpful
and defend us from whatever is harmful,
let us pray to the Lord:

+

+

Priest: Lord God, our need for your mercy is great,
but your kindness to us is far greater.
Receive these prayers we have made to you,
and answer them for the sake of your beloved
     Son, Jesus Christ,
who is Lord for ever and ever. Amen.

TWENTY-SECOND SUNDAY IN ORDINARY TIME

Priest: Let us call on the Lord's name
and offer fervent prayer for ourselves and for
all people.

Minister: For the ministers of all Christian churches,
that the Lord will uphold them
as they give their lives for the Gospel of
Christ,
let us pray to the Lord:

For public officials of this community, state,
and nation,
that the Lord will uphold them
as they work to protect our environment,
let us pray to the Lord:

For the poor, the hungry, and the homeless,
that the Lord will uphold them
by our assistance to them,
let us pray to the Lord:

For the sick and the elderly,
that the Lord will uphold them
by our care for them,
let us pray to the Lord:

For all who have died,
especially _____ and _____,
that the Lord will uphold them
in everlasting love,
let us pray to the Lord:

+

+

Priest: **Father of our Lord Jesus Christ,**
let us see your power and glory
in answer to these prayers.
Make us pleasing in your sight,
so that your will may be done in us and
     through us.
We ask this in the name of Jesus, the Lord.
     Amen.

September 1, 2008

LABOR DAY
(United States of America and Canada)

Priest: As we give thanks for the work that sustains
            our lives
         and fulfills God's plan for our world,
         let us offer these petitions to the God of
            mercy.

Minister: For the church,
         that it extend God's saving work to all nations,
         let us pray to the Lord:

         For workers in this and every land,
         that they enjoy respect, safety,
         and just compensation for their labor,
         let us pray to the Lord:

         For those who cannot find jobs or keep them,
         that they receive assistance in their need,
         let us pray to the Lord:

         For us who worship here,
         that we accomplish God's redemptive purpose
         in the many places of our work,
         let us pray to the Lord:

         For those who have died,
         especially _____ and _____,
         that they enjoy eternal rest with God,
         let us pray to the Lord:

+

+

Priest: **Lord God,
we ask you to answer these prayers,
so that we can bring the fullness of our
intelligence,
strength, and care to our work
and glorify you in all things.
We ask this through Jesus Christ, the Lord.
Amen.**

TWENTY-THIRD SUNDAY IN ORDINARY TIME

Priest: Let us join our voices and pray for each other's
needs
in Jesus' name.

Minister: For the well-being of the holy church of God,
and for the unity of all Christians,
let us pray to the Lord:

For peace in the world, and the reconciliation
of states and peoples,
let us pray to the Lord:

For the safety of students and teachers in our
schools,
let us pray to the Lord:

For the healing of the sick, the feeding of the
hungry,
and the consolation of the afflicted,
let us pray to the Lord:

For the eternal happiness of those who have
died,
especially _____ and _____,
let us pray to the Lord:

+

+

Priest: **God of our salvation,**
hear our prayers and watch over us always.
Guide us as your flock, and keep us safe in
**   your love.**
We ask this through Christ our Lord. Amen.

EXALTATION OF THE HOLY CROSS

Priest: The Lord Jesus humbled himself
and became obedient unto death,
even to death on a cross.
In the power of his resurrection from the
  dead,
let us pray that all people will be raised up
to new life in Christ the Lord.

Minister: Christ crucified became like us in our
  weakness;
through his Cross,
may the church become like him in his saving
  power.
For this, let us pray to the Lord:

Christ crucified became like the poor and the
  oppressed in their need;
through his Cross,
may they become like him in his triumph over
  injustice.
For this, let us pray to the Lord:

Christ crucified became like us in our sorrows;
through his Cross,
may all who suffer become like him in his
  lasting joy.
For this, let us pray to the Lord:

Christ crucified became like us in our human
      lowliness;
through his Cross,
may we become like him in his divine glory.
For this, let us pray to the Lord:

Christ crucified became like the dead in their
      emptiness;
through his Cross,
may those who have died,
especially _____ and _____,
become like him in his fullness of life.
For this, let us pray to the Lord:

+

+

Priest: Lord God,
answer our prayers in your great mercy,
so that the mystery of our redemption in the
      Cross of Christ
may transform us and the world you love.
We ask this through our crucified yet risen
      Savior,
Jesus Christ, who is Lord for ever and ever.
      Amen.

TWENTY-FIFTH SUNDAY IN ORDINARY TIME
(Catechetical Sunday)

Priest: Let us call on the Lord, who is near to us in every need.

Minister: For catechists and teachers of the Christian faith,
that they proclaim the Lord's greatness
in their service of God's people,
let us pray to the Lord:

For the leaders of governments,
that they reflect the Lord's greatness
in their work for victims of injustice,
let us pray to the Lord:

For those who suffer from sickness,
especially _____ and _____,
that they know the Lord's greatness
in words and deeds of compassion,
let us pray to the Lord:

For us who worship here,
that we imitate the Lord's greatness
in our love for others,
let us pray to the Lord:

For those who have died,
especially _____ and _____,
that they celebrate the Lord's greatness
in the gift of salvation,
let us pray to the Lord:

+

+

Priest: **Gracious God,
give answer to our prayers in your great
kindness.
Teach us your ways of love,
so that in all we do and say,
we will glorify your holy name.
We ask this through Christ our Lord. Amen.**

TWENTY-SIXTH SUNDAY IN ORDINARY TIME

Priest:　Confident that the Lord's kindness is
　　　　everlasting,
let us offer these petitions to the God of
　　　mercy.

Minister:　That the Lord's goodness
will empower the members of the church for
　　　generous service,
let us pray to the Lord:

That the Lord's guidance
will direct our public servants along the paths
　　　of justice and peace,
let us pray to the Lord:

That the Lord's salvation
will speedily deliver the people of this and
　　　every country
from poverty, starvation, and homelessness,
let us pray to the Lord:

That the Lord's compassion
will comfort the sick, the aged, and the dying,
let us pray to the Lord:

That the Lord's mercy
will embrace the lives of those who have died,
especially _____ and _____,
let us pray to the Lord:

+

+

Priest: **God our Savior,
your kindness embraces all peoples,
and your faithfulness knows no limits.
All our hope is in your mercy.
Answer our prayers for the sake of him
whose death shows us the way to life,
your Son, Jesus Christ.
He lives and reigns as Lord, for ever and ever.
Amen.**

October 5, 2008

TWENTY-SEVENTH SUNDAY
IN ORDINARY TIME
(Respect Life Sunday)

Priest: **With loving confidence, we now bring before
        the Lord
all the needs of the human family.**

Minister: **That faith may create in the church
a welcome for the prophets of life,
let us pray to the Lord:**

**That love may create in our society
a welcome for all the unborn,
let us pray to the Lord:**

**That mercy may create in our world
a welcome for the homeless and the hungry,
let us pray to the Lord:**

**That compassion may create in our
        communities
a welcome for the mentally and physically ill,
let us pray to the Lord:**

**That justice may create around the globe
a welcome for the socially and economically
        disadvantaged,
let us pray to the Lord:**

**That generosity may create in our nation's
        families
a welcome for adoptive children,
let us pray to the Lord:**

That divine love may create for those who
    have died,
especially _____ and _____,
a welcome into everlasting happiness,
let us pray to the Lord:

+

+

Priest: Lord God, Creator and Giver of life,
hear the prayers of your people.
Transform us in your love
so that your kingdom may grow in our midst.
We ask this through Christ our Lord. Amen.

TWENTY-EIGHTH SUNDAY IN ORDINARY TIME

Priest: **Let us turn to God in confident prayer, asking for what we need to live as a holy people.**

Minister: **That God's goodness will be a source of wisdom
for all the members of the church,
let us pray to the Lord:**

**That God's goodness will be a source of peace
for nations, peoples, and communities,
let us pray to the Lord:**

**That God's goodness will be a source of comfort
for those who suffer in mind, body, or spirit,
let us pray to the Lord:**

**That God's goodness will be a source of holiness for us
as we walk in the way of the Lord,
let us pray to the Lord:**

**That God's goodness will be a source of everlasting life
for those who have died,
especially _____ and _____,
let us pray to the Lord:**

+

+

Priest: **God of wisdom and love,**
you know our every need even before
**   we ask.**
Show us your goodness in answer to these
**   prayers,**
so that seeking your kingdom may be our joy.
We ask this through Christ our Lord. Amen.

TWENTY-NINTH SUNDAY IN ORDINARY TIME
(World Mission Sunday)

Priest: Let us present our prayers to the Lord,
whose kindness and mercy bring hope to all
the earth.

Minister: That missionaries will find renewed strength
in God's love,
let us pray to the Lord:

That all nations and peoples
will find lasting peace in God's plan for this
world,
let us pray to the Lord:

That the ill,
especially _____ and _____,
will find abundant comfort in God's healing,
let us pray to the Lord:

That all who worship here
will find sure guidance in God's Word,
let us pray to the Lord:

That those who have died,
especially _____ and _____,
will find everlasting joy in God's glory,
let us pray to the Lord:

+

+

Priest: **All-holy God,**
we ask you to answer our prayers,
for you are merciful and gracious to all your
      people.
Rescue us from whatever could harm us,
and crown us with your kindness and
      compassion in Christ Jesus,
both now and for ever. Amen.

October 26, 2008

THIRTIETH SUNDAY IN ORDINARY TIME

Priest: Let us call on our God,
who is compassionate toward us in our need.

Minister: For the welfare of the holy church of God,
and the unity of the human family,
let us pray to the Lord:

For peace throughout the world,
and the reconciliation of states and peoples,
let us pray to the Lord:

For the healing of the sick and the feeding of
the hungry,
let us pray to the Lord:

For our deliverance from all affliction and
danger,
let us pray to the Lord:

For everlasting light and peace for those who
have died,
especially _____ and _____,
let us pray to the Lord:

For our particular needs, which we now
remember.

[pause for silent prayer]

For all our needs, let us pray to the Lord:

+

+

Priest: **Lord, in your kindness, answer our prayers.**
Fill our hearts with the spirit of your charity,
that we may please you in our thoughts and
  actions
and love you in our sisters and brothers.
We ask this through Christ our Lord. Amen.

ALL SAINTS

Priest: Gathered in the holy presence of God,
let us pray for our world and for all who dwell
in it.

Minister: That the church will receive God's blessing
in its desire for holiness,
let us pray to the Lord:

That all nations will receive God's blessing
in freedom from injustice and war,
let us pray to the Lord:

That those who seek public office will receive
God's blessing
in promoting the common good,
let us pray to the Lord:

That those who suffer from poverty, illness,
and homelessness
will receive God's blessing in renewed hope,
let us pray to the Lord:

That this assembly of God's children will
receive God's blessing
in this sacrifice of thanksgiving,
let us pray to the Lord:

That those who have died,
especially _____ and _____,
will receive God's blessing in everlasting
glory,
let us pray to the Lord:

+

+

Priest:　With all the saints around your throne, O God,
we offer prayers that reach toward praise.
Let us rejoice and be glad in your love
as we celebrate life in the kingdom of your
　　Son, Jesus Christ,
who is Lord for ever and ever. Amen.

COMMEMORATION OF
ALL THE FAITHFUL DEPARTED
(All Souls)

Priest: **Blessed is the Lord our God,**
Ruler of life and death,
for raising the beloved Son as the firstborn
      from the dead.
In his life-giving name,
let us pray that all who sleep in Christ
will awake to share his glory.

Minister: **The Lord Jesus raised the widow's son to life.**
In his name, let us ask God's unending life
for our deceased relatives and friends.
For this, let us pray to the Lord:

The Lord Jesus wept for Lazarus
when he lay in the tomb.
In his name, let us ask God's consolation
for all who mourn.
For this, let us pray to the Lord:

The Lord Jesus promised paradise
to the repentant thief.
In his name, let us ask God's happiness
for all who died in great misery and suffering.
For this, let us pray to the Lord:

The Lord Jesus fed the hungry and healed the
sick.
In his name, let us ask God's refreshment
for victims of war, neglect, starvation, and
disease.
For this, let us pray to the Lord:

The Lord Jesus sought the good of his people.
In his name, let us ask God's wisdom
for those who will vote on Tuesday
and for those who will be elected.
For this, let us pray to the Lord:

The Lord Jesus redeemed his faithful ones
through the Cross.
In his name, let us ask God's salvation
for our fellow parishioners who have died,
especially _____ and _____,
and for all God's servants.
For this, let us pray to the Lord:

+

+

Priest: Holy, immortal God,
you are the source of everlasting life for all
your people.
Grant forgiveness and peace
to those whom we remember today at your
altar.
We ask this in the name of Jesus the Lord.
Amen.

DEDICATION OF THE LATERAN BASILICA IN ROME

Priest: We are God's building,
the living stones rising on a firm foundation
in Christ Jesus.
In the power of the Holy Spirit who dwells
within us,
let us offer fervent prayers to the Lord.

Minister: That the church will gather into one
the scattered children of God throughout the
world,
let us pray to the Lord:

That believers of all religions
will be able to worship God in freedom and
peace,
let us pray to the Lord:

That architects, designers, and artists will use
their talents
to reveal the glory of God,
let us pray to the Lord:

That we who render devoted service to God in
this Eucharist
will render generous help to our needy
brothers and sisters,
let us pray to the Lord:

That all who have died,
especially _____ and _____,
will find a dwelling place in God's eternal
     home,
let us pray to the Lord:

+

+

Priest: **Lord God, wise builder of your church,**
we ask you to answer the prayers
we have offered in your holy house.
Raise us to share the everlasting glory of your
    risen Son,
Jesus Christ, who is Lord for ever and ever.
    Amen.

THIRTY-THIRD SUNDAY IN ORDINARY TIME

Priest: As children of the day, who face life with
      hope,
let us pray to God with confidence.

Minister: For the church,
that God may protect and prosper it
      throughout the world,
let us pray to the Lord:

For civil authorities,
that God may direct them along the ways of
      all that is good,
let us pray to the Lord:

For those among us who are suffering in mind
      or body,
that God may deliver them from pain and
      distress,
let us pray to the Lord:

For this assembly,
that God may empower us to build a more
      humane world,
let us pray to the Lord:

For those who have gone before us
in the discipleship of Christ,
especially _____ and _____,
that God may grant them refreshment, light,
      and peace,
let us pray to the Lord:

+

+

Priest: **Gracious God, giver of all good gifts,**
hear our prayers,
so that we may rejoice in the breadth of your
kindness
and the depth of your mercy.
We ask this through Christ our Lord. Amen.

OUR LORD JESUS CHRIST THE KING

Priest: Let us ask God to hear and answer our
                    prayers,
              which we offer in union with Christ our King.

Minister: That God's people will serve Christ the King
              by caring for the spiritual and physical needs
                    of his least ones,
              let us pray to the Lord:

              That leaders of governments will recognize
                    the rights of the oppressed
              and honor the dignity of all,
              let us pray to the Lord:

              That Jesus will come quickly
              to save those who wait in suffering, pain, and
                    despair,
              let us pray to the Lord:

              That we who worship here
              will know the goodness and kindness of the
                    Lord at this table,
              let us pray to the Lord:

              That those who have died,
              especially _____ and _____,
              will find everlasting joy around God's throne,
              let us pray to the Lord:

+

+

Priest: Almighty and eternal God,
you willed to renew and restore all things in
your beloved Son,
the King of the universe.
Help us to live the truth of his kingship
by serving our sisters and brothers with our
whole heart.
We ask this through Christ our Lord. Amen.

THANKSGIVING DAY
(United States of America)

Priest: God has cared for our nation from its
beginning,
but God has always invited us to pray.
On this day of grateful celebration,
let us offer our petitions.

Minister: For those who are called to ministry in the
church,
that they work for its unity and peace,
let us pray to the Lord:

For those who serve in public office,
that they lead us with love for justice,
let us pray to the Lord:

For all who produce food for the world,
that they receive a just return for their labor,
let us pray to the Lord:

For all who work for the well-being of the
human family,
that they rejoice in the hope they give to
others,
let us pray to the Lord:

For the sick of our community,
especially _____ and _____,
that we surround them with our love and
compassion,
let us pray to the Lord:

For ourselves and those dear to us,
that we find strength in our mutual love,
let us pray to the Lord:

For those who have died,
especially _____ and _____,
that they sing the everlasting song of
    thanksgiving in heaven,
let us pray to the Lord:

+

+

Priest: Almighty Father,
in these prayers we open our hands
to receive your abundant gifts,
and we open our hearts to share them with
    others.
Bless our receiving and our giving,
we humbly ask,
for we call out in the name of Jesus,
who is Lord for ever and ever. Amen.